The Death and Rebirth of Ophelia

The Death and Rebirth of Ophelia

Poems by

Robert Cooperman

© 2025 Robert Cooperman. All rights reserved.
This material may not be reproduced in any form, published,
reprinted, recorded, performed, broadcast,
rewritten, or redistributed without
the explicit permission of Robert Cooperman.
All such actions are strictly prohibited by law.

Cover design by Shay Culligan
Cover photo of Ophelia, courtesy of Dalton Smith
Author photo by Beth Cooperman

ISBN: 978-1-63980-705-5

Kelsay Books
502 South 1040 East, A-119
American Fork, Utah 84003
Kelsaybooks.com

*for Herman Asarnow, Hugh Ruppersburg,
and in Loving Memory, John Vance*

and as always, for Beth, my Portia

Acknowledgments

The author wishes to thank the editors of the following journals, where some of these poems, in earlier forms, first appeared:

California Quarterly: "The Player King and His Troupe Leave the Court of Elsinore"
The Pangolin Review: "Claudius Views the Drowned Corpse of Ophelia"
The Raven's Perch: "Ophelia Fakes Her Own Drowning," "Cunegunde, the Strolling Player Who Changes Places with Ophelia, Is Killed by Hamlet," "Horatio Views 'Ophelia's' Corpse," "Claudius Views the Drowned Corpse of Ophelia"

Contents

I—A Corpse in the Court of Elsinore

Ophelia Fakes Her Own Drowning	15
Cunegunde, the Strolling Player Who Changes Places with Ophelia, Is Killed by Hamlet	17
Hamlet, After "Ophelia's" Drowning	19
Horatio Views "Ophelia's" Corpse	22
The Player King and His Troupe Leave the Court of Elsinore	24
Claudius Views the Drowned Corpse of Ophelia	25
Gertrude Observes Ophelia's Corpse	27
Laertes Views the Corpse	29
The Ghost of Hamlet's Father, as "Ophelia" Is About to Be Buried	31
Polonius' Ghost Views the Corpse of "Ophelia"	34
The Grave Digger Fills in "Ophelia's" Grave	36

II—In the Company of the Strolling Players

Ophelia Travels with the Band of Strolling Players	41
The Player King Observes the Woman He Thinks of as Cunegunde	44
Griselda Considers the Woman Who Calls Herself Cunegunde	46
Ophelia Considers Griselda	49
In a Quiet Moment, Ophelia Thinks of Hamlet's Killing of Her Father, Polonius	51
Feste the Clown and Lute Player Thinks of "Cunegunde"	53 53
Gunnar Considers the Play, *The Mousetrap*	56
Ophelia Hears of the Deaths of Her Brother Laertes and Her Former Lover Hamlet	58

Ophelia Ponders the Death of Queen Gertrude	60
Fortinbras, King of Norway, Commands the Player King's Troupe to Perform for Him	62
Ophelia, as Cunegunde, Thinks of Fortinbras	65
Isaak, Another Member of the Troupe of Traveling Players	67
Samson, the Traveling Acting Troupe's Strongman	69
Isaak Remembers What Drew Him to the Actor's Life	71
Ophelia, as Cunegunde, Considers Isaak	73
Griselda Plots the Downfall of Ophelia	75
Griselda and the Vial of Poison	78
Griselda Returns the Vial of Poison to the Crone	81

III—Such Strength of Love

Gunnar Learns the Truth About the Woman He Thought Was Cunegunde	85
Fortinbras Confronts Ophelia	87
Ophelia Rejects the Offer of King Fortinbras	89
Ophelia, After Rejecting the Suit of King Fortinbras	92
Ophelia Counsels Griselda, After the Latter's First Performance in the Strolling Troupe	95
King Fortinbras to Gunnar	97
Gunnar, After Being Confronted by King Fortinbras	99
Samson Thinks of Griselda	101
Griselda Thinks of Samson	102
Ophelia Considers Her New Life	104

I—A Corpse in the Court of Elsinore

Ophelia Fakes Her Own Drowning

After Hamlet insulted my virtue yet again,
and me giving him my all and gladly,
I ran sobbing to the Lower Town,
there glimpsed a female strolling player.

I gasped: my visage in a still pond's surface,
She drew back as if from some devilment,
but when I stammered we should exchange places,
she was a hound slobbering over that meaty bone,
dreaming of lolling at Elsinore's court forever.

And me? I wished but to escape my mad prince:
not just his constant volleys of insults,
but the not so small matter of the unwanted flower
he planted in me by the rich soil of the riverbank.

One of my maids had whispered of a witch
whose chimney smoke is a beacon for all
who find themselves in such difficulties.
After I availed myself of her potions,
I rehearsed bawdy badinage before tavern-peasants,
their shouts and tossed coins at my ribaldry
all the proof I needed I could play the thespian.

Even that drab's brother demanded
why wasn't I in costume as the Virgin,
for their next court performance.

Now, wind carries the sad news
that wench, Cunegunde, has drowned,
fish-nibbled, unrecognizable, except
for the gown I exchanged for
her gypsy kirtle and blouse. I'd wager
that my former betrothed slew her:
his rages uncontrollable as a weather cock
flung about by Ultima Thule's
perpetual winter storms.

Christ only knows the kingdom's fate
if Hamlet's madness continues unchecked:
my poor father the only brake on his choler,
and look how the Prince's dagger rewarded him.

Though I confess as our troupe
wagon-creaks away, I care not a fig
for the rot rising from Elsinore.

Cunegunde, the Strolling Player Who Changes Places with Ophelia, Is Killed by Hamlet

When Lady Ophelia accosted me—
us as alike as two lambs
from the same ewe—I wanted
to run from the witchcraft,
then realized she had a proposal:

her tear-bloated unhappiness
plain as a play script, even if
I can't read, and anyway, far better
than remembering my lines,
my glorious titties, worth
their weight in gold
when I bare them to the howling
approval of the men in audiences.

"What's in it for me?" I bluffed,
knowing the rewards, and besides,
playing a court lady in real life,
the role of a lifetime.

Then there was Hamlet,
a handsome, well-born sod
who'd marry me church-legal,
so I could escape our troupe's leader,
his kisses greasy, his hands sloppy
as suet, when he slid sausage-fingers
down my bosoms and thighs,
though his roving hands were useful
to get me the place of honor
in our stroller's troupe.

But compared to his slipshod coupling,
I thought to live fairy-tale happy,
dropping Hamlet babies
and whispering how to get rid
of his uncle, who, rumors froth,
killed Hamlet's sire
and stole the throne and the love
of the Prince's boisterous dam.

Except I didn't reckon on
Ophelia's vixen-shaped birthmark,
whereas my thigh was unblemished,
so Hamlet accused I'd murdered her.

I tried to fight him off
with the dagger I always keep hidden,
but he was crazed, his soft hands
choking me into dark silence.

When I hit the water, I came to,
but never could swim, and besides,
My Lady's gown and petticoats
dragged me under, like a rock
tossed by a sullen schoolboy:

all my dreams vanishing
in choking bubbles.

Hamlet, After "Ophelia's" Drowning

The first time, I had to coax
and cajole Ophelia to open
her wet treasure to me,
but after she crawled back
from the Lower Town and her bout
of tears over my pretending
to order her to a house
of carnal recreation,

she was an eager strumpet,
performing acts I'd gaped at,
from Horatio's confiding,
after his visit to a palace
of horizontal exercise.

I assumed she'd pored over
French manuals
at a bawdy bookseller's
my head a madly spinning top
at the creamy pleasure
throbbing from me.

But the truth came out
when she plucked off her robe
for the main course:
Ophelia's thigh birthmark,
that I'd love to trace
with a lazy forefinger
after we'd done the deed,
vanished.

"What have you done
to Ophelia?" I shouted,
fearing the jade had slain her
to profit from the resemblance
and to murder me,
at Claudius' distant direction,
and indeed her dagger slashed
far too close to my ear
for my liking.

My hands flew to her throat;
she struggled, and to my shame,
my peggo was straining:
a hound hunting an escaped
villein's terrified scent.
At her last strangled gasp,
I soiled myself and her,
then after sobbing a moment,
yanked her gown back down
over her bosom and thighs,
tossed her into the river,
and played the grief-mad swain
when her corpse washed up.

Of course no one noticed
the absence of the birthmark,
under the guise of covering
her modesty in death.

I keep telling myself
she was only a strumpet,
and had killed Ophelia
or coerced my darling
into trading places,
so this trollop could profit
by easy court life,
and even more,
by duping me into thinking
she was my beloved Ophelia.

Horatio Views "Ophelia's" Corpse

It took me but an instant to see
she wasn't my Lady Ophelia:
an uncharacteristic smirk
even in death, her color
too outdoor-tawny,
her fingernails jagged
and toil-muddy.

From the marks ringing
her throat, she hadn't drowned,
but was murdered, probably
by Hamlet, for whatever reason
I'd no idea and didn't want to know,

merely had to cover it up,
so the court wouldn't suffer
yet another catastrophe
of his melancholy mania:
my sworn duty to protect my friend,
especially from himself.

Had this imposter
dispatched Ophelia for gain?
Or, I thought, more likely
they'd switched lives.
I'd wager My Lady
had absconded with that troupe
of players at dawn,

and this one, whoever she was,
had lost the bargain, poor drab,
thinking she'd won an easy
court life as the Prince's consort,
so long as she played her role
every instant of every day and night.

But that's impossible, as she learned.
Hamlet may be off-kilter
as a slowing top, or merely
feigning lunacy, but he always
notices everything.

A fast rider could overtake that troupe,
fetch Ophelia back to her rightful place,
but that would make the Prince's life
even more complicated,
and hers unbearable again.

Better to let her escape
this cursed court and mad Hamlet.

The Player King and His Troupe Leave the Court of Elsinore

What a stink sulphured up
from that court's sewers,
the shit from all the demons of Hell.
In the future we'll skirt past that fen,
no matter how fat the purse
the mad Prince or his treacherously
affable uncle, the King, tosses us.

Even worse, I had to bite my tongue
and nod when Hamlet instructed me,
*Me! o*n the players' craft:

"I pray thee, speak the lines trippingly,"
the pedant! As if I'd never recited
a speech. How else should one speak them,
mumbling out the side of one's mouth?
Stuttering like a simpleton, so no one
in the audience can make out a word?

Inwardly, I was an Icelandic
fire mountain, me, lauded by kings,
poets, and fellow players in Stockholm
and Uppsala, tutored by a backwater
princeling dilettante!

Still, the troupe admirably performed
the play he commanded,
though so many more
interesting ones in our repertoire.

Claudius Views the Drowned Corpse of Ophelia

Obvious as a Swedish strumpet,
she didn't commit self-murder
and risk the eternal damnation
I'd face, if I believed in such nonsense
for killing my brother and usurping
his throne, then besmirching his bed
with his widow, night after delicious night.

And even before, when my older,
officious brother would be away
on court business, maybe to Norway,
maybe to Sweden or Hanover,
while he left me in charge of Elsinore,
where I indulged in my lust for riding out
on a fine stallion to hunt the stag and boar
and my even greater lust for Gertrude.

She was wasted on my brother, more monk
than man, a wonder he managed
to produce an heir on my plum-luscious
bedmate. And in truth, we were enjoying
his absences even in the early days
of their union, perhaps the Mad Prince
is my issue, though I shudder to think so.

But back to this latest murder:
the bruises necklacing her throat proof
Ophelia was not a despairing flower
scorned by the high-born whoreson
she'd given her heart and priceless ruby to,
and still grieving for her father,
but murdered on a lark by my nephew,
his Humours so out of balance
a wonder he can walk a straight line.

But Ophelia's death plays into my hands,
simple for a court councilor
to regretfully find the evidence
to execute the meddler-Prince.
Who knows, maybe she refused him,
or worse, welcomed his loins' quickening,
thus proving, to his confused mind,
she was a harlot deserving
a murderous exit from the earth.

In any case, he's given me
the means to be rid of him;
not even his mother—
who, I secretly smile,
grows more tired
of his erratic behavior by the day—
will plead for leniency or excuse
his conduct as boyish antics.

At his age, I was hatching plots
like clever vipers, of taking
the throne by guile or force
from my smugly virtuous brother.

A good thing I'm a patient man,
for it took so long for desire
and opportunity to merge into action.

Gertrude Observes Ophelia's Corpse

Though clad in Ophelia's gown,
the corpse was from that troupe
of strolling players that left
this morning with full purses
from my generous-to-a-fault son.

The "River of Tears" had switched
lives with her, or dare I dream it,
this jade murdered Ophelia,
to bask in court life, yoked
to my indulgent princely boy,
the drab tiring of treading the boards.

Ophelia's tears drove Hamlet mad,
and when I observed she was with issue,
her sobs insisted it was my son's.

"Liar! Harlot!" I slapped her.

"What you don't know about your angel
would fill a hymnal," she snapped,
for once showing a little spirit.

Beneath her Easter-lily timidity,
she cocooned my son
to her every whining whim
and now has absconded or is dead;
only Christ knows or cares,
and this simulacrum's drowned.
Good riddance to the pair
of plotting Salomes.

Should Ophelia ever return
from her wanderings
or from "the unexplored country"—
poets' outlandish metaphor
for the Hell she's earned—
her resurrection will be brief.

Laertes Views the Corpse

This slattern bears
a passing resemblance
to my darling sister,
but where Ophelia
was lamb-soft,
this one smirks hard
as the peggo
she no doubt craved.

Seeing this harlot,
I know my lily-sister lives
under Christ's blue sky,
though the Mad Prince
may hold her prisoner
to his filthy desires
in a secret chamber,
substituting this drab
so I'll quietly mourn.

After the others withdraw,
murmuring condolences
at the death of a paragon-maiden,
I'll question Hamlet
with my dagger,
to ensure he speaks true:
no more of his running
fox circles 'round me,
with his witty words
that signify nothing,
but make him feel clever
at my expense.

If he lies, the Prince will taste
my blade: all his cunning
running red from his throat,
just vengeance
for his sword silencing
my poor Father,
who, I confess, drove me mad
with his constant advice.

Hamlet will tell me where he's hid
my dear sister, and confess
all the unspeakable abominations
he's perpetrated on her,
or he'll join this strumpet
he no doubt employed,
who from her visage
was more than willing
to enjoy his liberties
on her too-ripe flesh.

But I confess,
were I not in a rage
and if she weren't cold
as a bled hog, this one
would've been to my tastes:
a shame Hamlet ended
her honest whoring.

The Ghost of Hamlet's Father, as "Ophelia" Is About to Be Buried

In life, I was too consumed
with matters of state
to notice my brother and wife
clawing at each other
like minks in rut, let alone
consider the possibility
their writhings might be
a prelude to regicide.

Obvious this corpse
isn't Ophelia, for I'd often
smiled at the sweet girl,
engaged her in chit-chat,
gently teased her
about doting on my son,
though I thought her perhaps
a touch too simple for him.

But she's changed places
with this one: proving me
wrong to call her naive,
when all she wanted
was to be free
of our festering court,
while this simulacrum
lusted for a soft life
with my son, who slew her
the instant he thought
she'd killed Ophelia.

If only he'd be that ruthless
with my darling brother.
Instead, Hamlet dithers, stabs
good, if garrulous, Polonius
almost on a whim, plays
coy games with grim Claudius
over that drama my get forced
that troupe to perform:
a tragedy that all but accused
my loving brother of incest,
treason, and murder,
and will surely goad him
into ridding himself of Hamlet,

while my philosophical simpleton
of a son questions himself
as to why he can't thrust a dagger
through my sweet brother's throat.

Yes, please explain that to me,
Hamlet, you metaphysical oaf!

More reason to admire Ophelia,
climbing out of, away from,
this sewer that calls itself
a royal court.

Oh that I could leave as well,
not be forced to witness
my honorable brother
and virtuous wife fornicating,
or to despair over my son's
eternal blatherings,
when he should avenge
his best-of-all fathers,
so I can ascend
to some semblance of Heaven.

Polonius' Ghost Views the Corpse of "Ophelia"

This is not my daughter,
but a demon-changeling,
a succubus that has taken on
a passing resemblance
to my pure and obedient girl.

In life, I advised the king,
his feckless son, and my own
headstrong lad, who had
as much use for words
and rational thought
as a strolling strongman
for a volume of sermons
except to prove his puissance
by tearing it in half.

Now, I merely hover, fail—
with all my invisible flailings
and futile attempts
to knock over chairs, tables,
blow out torch flames
lodged in wall sconces
when there's no wind—

to make living mourners
suspect an outraged ghost
is at work and to see
this creature lying before them
is a shape shifter that's stolen
my darling's likeness,
a fiend that lies silent, heavy,
not virtuous enough to rise
to a gossamer-flitting existence.

And again, where is my daughter?
Could she fear to show herself:
her father no longer alive
to protect her with my wise counsel,
her brother still so besotted,
from his wallowing sojourn
in Paris' bagnios and taverns
that he thought me a simpleton
to confuse those dens
of harlots and panderers
with the lecture halls
of the Sorbonne?

The Grave Digger Fills in "Ophelia's" Grave

Poor Lady Ophelia,
finally finding your true home:
as a child you always played
among the graves,
weaving bouquets, claiming,
with a child's certainty,

"Flowers will help them
feel less lonely."

When I showed you
my wife's and daughter's graves—
old King Hamlet granting me
leave to bury my dear ones
among the quality—
you took my paw
in your princess fingers
and asked,

"Do you think they're happy?"
a frown furrowing
your pitying brow.

"Yes," I smiled,
but wanted to answer,
"happier than I am or will be,
'til I join them."

We returned to my shack,
where I brewed tea
and we played draughts.
Another time I wove a tale
of a great prince
who'd sweep you up
on his gentle stallion,
take you to his palace
in a far off magic land,
marry you, and make you
happy forever.

Little did I know
he'd be mad Hamlet,
whose sneers drove you
to the river's
cold embrace.

How much more content
you'd have been as my daughter,
marrying my young successor,
bearing his bairns, cooking,
keeping your cottage trim
as a ship's galley: a good,
rewarding life, far
from our cursed court.

But something's amiss,
your sweet sadness replaced
by the sharp features
of a trickster trollop:
maybe just that the river's
cold arms have hardened you.

Or maybe what some whisper
about you and that strolling harlot
trading places is true:
If so, I rejoice you're still upright,
but mourn this poor lass,
who may have been no better
than she should be, but didn't
deserve to pay for her wantonness
with her brief life.

II—In the Company of the Strolling Players

Ophelia Travels with the Band of Strolling Players

We women strollers do far more
than tread the boards and collect coins
from a pleased audience at play's end.
We gather wood, build fires, cook meals,
and assure male players their performances
would delight Christ Himself, let alone
the peasants who laugh and weep
to be freed from their hard lives
for the duration of a drama or comedy.

Afraid the others will suspect
I'm not their comrade Cunegunde,
I haul kindling and logs, skin
and gut rabbits, and bargain
for chickens from farmers, letting
the leering louts stare long and hungrily
down my bodice, and take a liberty or two,
to cheapen the price, and try not to shudder
at their filthy, slug-fat fingers.

As for the men in our troupe,
when not strutting and sweating the stage,
they swagger off to taverns, drink, boast,
game, squeeze breasts as if testing melons,
and press their padded codpieces against
the bellies of wenches, whether they welcome
the mock impalings or not.

Still, I'd never return to Elsinore,
to endure Hamlet's venomed jests,
or his dithering at taking vengeance
on Claudius, so tired I've become
of his endless whining over whether
to kill the usurper or himself,
all but impossible not to scream at him,

"Oh, just cease to be,
and leave the rest of us in peace!"

And worst of all, he murdered Father.
Don't tell me it was an accident,
a momentary fit of madness.
He knew who was behind the arras,
and was punishing me for shutting
my door to his loathsome advances.

What makes my sojourn
among these rag-tags bearable,
even a pleasure?
My getting to pretend
to be someone else
when I take to the boards.

Even better, there's Feste,
the troupe's clown and lutenist,
his bawdy ditties cascading
glad tears down my cheek,
and the only male in our troupe
who hasn't tried to thrust
his fleshy engine at me,
while backing me against
a tree trunk, as if a Sabine woman
enslaved on a Roman raid.

The Player King Observes the Woman He Thinks of as Cunegunde

She no longer guides
my hands to knead
her breasts and thighs,
nor wiggles her buttocks
against my saluting peggo,
nor does she suffer me
entrance into her portal of joy.

Something happened to her
during our cursed sojourn
in Elsinore: once a frolicsome
harlot who could barely
remember a line longer than,
"Zounds," or "Swive me,
I pray thee, my randy lord!"

Now, when she speaks
some minor lines,
she's so lifelike I forget
she's a player treading the boards.
So I give her bigger parts
in our repertoire,
and by Jupiter's beard,
she's suddenly a natural.

She's been inspired,
I suspect, by a paramour,
some callow bumbler
who dotes on her and gasps
when she spreads herself
before him, naked and glorious
as the full moon; one
of the bumpkins, I'll wager,
who gawked when we performed,
and now follows my troupe,
but not close enough to raise
a pillar of dust I'd detect
and dispatch him with my dagger.

I fear she gives me poppy draughts
at night, so she can run barefoot
to him, to rut like swine,
like snakes, like worms,

though some in my company
have whispered she's not Cunegunde,
but that court lady, Ophelia,
we witnessed being upbraided
by the Demon Prince of Elsinore,
the two jades as alike—
some gawped—as issue
spilling from the same womb
mere instants apart.

A fine piece of theater, that!
But in real life? A steaming
pile of mare droppings.

Griselda Considers the Woman Who Calls Herself Cunegunde

How do I know
she's not Cunegunde?
That bitch never lifted
a finger at chores.
This one volunteers
for everything: desperate
to fit in and hide
from whatever's nipping
at her arse like a pack of wolves.

As Gunnar's favorite,
Cunegunde lolled
like Elizabeth Bathoray
in her tub of virgin's blood;
when she performed,
she never got her lines right,
or even delivered half
of them at all,
not that the men in the crowds
cared, since all they saw
was her squeezing her tits
the size of melons,
to raise a roar,
the fucking tease.

This one, though
the resemblance
is like two pine combs
from the same limb,
never needs a hissed prompt,
and carries herself
like a nun at her duties,
except, of course
when accosted by Gunnar,
our self-proclaimed Player King.

I saw her with my own
astonished eyes, slap him
when he tried to grab her coconuts;
and he too astounded to drag her
back to his wagon
for some rough recreation
I wouldn't mind at all,

When we played Elsinore,
I glimpsed a court lady
I thought was Cunegunde.
One of our men said she was Ophelia:
tormented relentlessly by Hamlet,
though once his beloved.

Maybe she fled his dagger-tongue
by joining us; and our Cunegunde
would've done anything
to barnacle herself
to a prince, even half-mad Hamlet.
We got the better of the trade,
so why can't I warm to this one,
so anxious to please?

It's the eternal envy
of the plain-faced
for the fair one
Gunnar favors,
always glazed over
by a pretty, simpering face
and the big downy breasts
men can't enough of.

Ophelia Considers Griselda

I've no idea how or why
I've earned her hatred;
maybe I try too hard to please,
afraid I'll be banished
from the safety of this troupe,
making its creaking-cart way
from the curse and rot
of Elsinore.

I so resembled their Cunegunde
I hoped they'd accept me
without a thought.

But she was said to exercise
a beauty's birthright of tyranny,
as well as being Gunnar's
pampered favorite: if not
for her performances on the boards
then in his thunder-thumping bed.

Sated by his attentions
and he off in villages and towns
arranging for the troupe
to play a town square
and for their nightly accommodations,
she'd order the others to bring
her delicacies and heady red wine:
more Jezebel than mild Ruth,
which is what I am or try to be.

Perhaps I should've eased into
my natural role, after I'd at first
played the imperious Queen
born to Beauty's crown
and all its privileges.

But I am who I am,
and can change only
when I tread the boards
and become someone
so different from myself,
it steals my breath
for an instant before I begin
to speak and metamorphose
into an utter and fascinating
stranger to myself.

In a Quiet Moment, Ophelia Thinks of Hamlet's Killing of Her Father, Polonius

Hamlet, you murderous fiend
who slew my dear Papa
on a whim, a jape.

Once, I'd have followed you
to Ultima Thule or to the wind-
biting deserts of Araby;
I lay with you in a bower of love
beside the river before you turned
merrily heartless: spat insults
at me as if a harlot who'd robbed you
of your purse and tainted you
with the pox.

Accursed creature,
you murdered a harmless old man,
who lived to give sage,
if sometimes rambling, advice,
who longed for Denmark to prosper,
for his beloved daughter
to be happily wed, and to see
his son calm his wild ways.

Now, Papa is cold flesh
in cold ground,
and Hamlet, why weren't you
more like your own father
in his unfailing courtesy,
always curious to hear
my opinion on big things
and little, and not merely
because you and I
were betrothed from childhood?

How I wish you'd been poisoned
by Claudius, instead of your father,
so that even at this remove,
I'd know Papa's still bestowing
kindly-meant advice
to all he comes across.

Let Laertes bury his sword
deep in your black heart,
you, whom once I loved,
and now can't abide
that we breathe the same air.

Feste the Clown and Lute Player Thinks of "Cunegunde"

Since Elsinore, she's no longer arrogant
in her beauty, but gentle and genteel,
as if upbraided by Our Lady,
on how a woman with her gifts
of face and form should comport herself.

I'd worshipped her with brooches,
necklaces, and bracelets of my own fashioning.
She'd sneer they lacked a master's stamp.
As for my lute-led serenades, she'd scowl,

"The shrieks of small, tortured animals."

But now, she smiles, nods, and taps her feet
whenever I stroke a melody on my lute
and make up lyrics as I go along.

"How lovely!" she'll clap her small hands,
beg for another, Gunnar
no longer summoning her:
the whole company heard the slap
she delivered when he tried
to get behind her and cup her breasts.
She wheeled on him like a swordsman,
no one able to contain their gaiety
at seeing him so upbraided.

When her palm lashed out,
he fell backward, like a bit
of rehearsed stage business
guaranteed to earn a laugh,

but I feared he might strike her
with a closed fist, for disobeying
his fleshly demands,
his right according to his lights
that, as our leader, he can take
whichever wench he desires.

If he had, I'd have hit him
with my lute, and gladly ruined
my career as a strolling player
had he ordered me away.
But he grabbed another player,
Griselda, who gloried to let him
shove her up the steps
of his pleasure wagon.

Shortly thereafter, Cunegunde
found me sitting alone in a grove.
She stroked my cheek and confided,

"I'm not who you think I am."

"You're the Lady Ophelia," I whispered
as if afraid anyone could hear us.
She kissed me, feather-soft.

So in all likelihood, Cunegunde
was dead, trying to pass as Ophelia.
I didn't know to cry from joy
at my new love, or for grief
that the woman I thought I'd loved
was so cruelly removed from the earth.

Afterwards, I strummed my lute
and made up words to songs
I invented on the spot, Ophelia
joining in on the choruses
we improvised together.

Gunnar Considers the Play, *The Mousetrap*

When the Idiot Prince demanded
we perform his revised version
of *The Murder of Gonzago,*
and added scenes to draw out
the guilt of King Claudius,
and re-titled it, *The Mousetrap*—
the title far better than the play
that Hamlet the Great had penned—
I thought it the most spectacularly
limp piece of theater I'd ever had
the misfortune to play.

Poison in the king's ear? Why not—
if he insisted on the ridiculous—
just piss into his nose! Aside from
Claudius and Hamlet, the crowd
could barely stifle their laughter:
husbands winking at wives, wives
giving husbands' tools a friendly stroke.

Later, my troupe fell down laughing
when I proposed adding my revised
stage business to our repertoire:
even Ophelia—or Cunegunde,
or whatever she called herself that week—
tittered, finally free of Hamlet's barbs,
and happy with her new love, Feste.

He's welcome to her, the jade refusing
my tupping, not like Cunegunde—
Christ rest her soul—burning for
my red rooster even before she tossed
off her robe and petticoat, though alas,
she was no Ophelia, who can play
anything and make it sound like
she was born to the role.

Too bad there's one role she refuses.

Ophelia Hears of the Deaths of Her Brother Laertes and Her Former Lover Hamlet

My poor headstrong brother,
believing swords could solve
any dilemma. It wasn't even me
you sought to avenge, dueling
with Hamlet, but Cunegunde,
one of the strolling players.

Even you couldn't have told us
apart; she lusted for court life
and I to escape Hamlet,
so we traded places.
The poor girl had no idea,
nor would she have cared
how much more corrupt
was Elsinore than a plague of rats.

All she wanted was to be pampered,
showered with gifts,
and become the consort
of a man she thought
one day might rule Denmark,
if Claudius could be slain,
or at the least imprisoned
or banished somewhere
so far away he could never
make his way back.

But now, you Laertes,
Cunegunde, and dear Papa
are slain by Hamlet,
a curse to all.
At least you killed him.

As children, whenever boys
yanked my braids or, older,
when courtiers insulted my honour
with their rapier insults inspired
by Hamlet's barbs, you roared
to my defense with drawn daggers
or swords: I smiled to see them beg,
rather than taste your steel.
Now, I have gentle Feste,
genteel without being born
to the lord and lady of a manor.

I grieve that Hamlet has killed you,
dear brother, though at least the cur
can no longer steal any more
of my dear ones.
May we meet in Heaven,
and have the pleasure of gazing
down, to see Hamlet in Hell.

Ophelia Ponders the Death of Queen Gertrude

You'd think, at the least,
I'd delight in her death:
Gertrude mocking me
for a whining lapdog
denied its treat, whenever
her son tongue-rapiered me,
the unwitting pawn in his plot
to avenge his father.

The last time Gertrude simpered
I protested over-much,
I was tempted to stab her
with my lady-dagger,
then inquire—demure
as a kitten licking its paws
of mouse blood—
whether that pained her.
But I tethered my rage.

Still, I tired of playing
Hamlet's lily-frail victim,
so when confronted
by my simulacrum
in the person of Cunegunde,
I traded places with her,
the strolling player
wild to swan about
as a great court lady,
and I desperate to escape
the hell of Elsinore.

But now, I see Gertrude
as merely a proud, fond mother,
who perhaps suspected
her first, noble lord
was murdered
by his blackguard brother, who,
she might have begun to fear,
would feel less of a prick
of conscience
to send her to Heaven
than in flicking
a bothersome fly
off his velvet sleeve,
should a younger, more
voluptuous kitten purr
a catalogue of the pleasures
awaiting him,
were she his royal consort.

So I grieve her, remember
how she'd smile, give me
honeyed confections, call me
"Dear Girl," and bid me play
children's games with her darling:

in her eyes, the two of us
already happily wed.

Fortinbras, King of Norway, Commands the Player King's Troupe to Perform for Him

King of great and glorious Norway
and now of Denmark, and without
losing a man to sword or pike,
though I'd have welcomed a battle,
to avenge my father's defeat and death
in war with Old Hamlet.
When I and my courtiers rode out
to survey my new prize,
we came upon a troupe of players,
so I demanded some bawdy fare.

"Batter me with tragedy," I warned,
"after the carnage I witnessed at Elsinore—
corpses like plague-slain rats—
or with clever, mocking philosophy,
like that mincing spigot of sarcasm,
Hamlet, and I'll reduce your troupe to ashes."

They put on an amusing farce: a buffoon
doting on the Queen of the Fairies;
her consort, to keep the high-born wench
in her place, transforming her dolt-paramour
into an ass she finds irresistible,
planting kisses on his snout
and stroking his pizzle. I laughed
'til tears coursed like the spring spate,
and tossed the players purses fat
as bulls' balls.

But one female had me gaping:
a jade named Cunegunde, for all
I could tell, a twin to the late
Lady Ophelia, sadly self-drowned
after that sarcastic git Hamlet
drove her to the river.
I'd met the sweet lady once,
when we were youths; she doted
on Hamlet, and I could only gawp
a lad's awe at the beauty she was.

When I questioned this Cunegunde—
for the sake of the love I once showered
silently on Ophelia—if she'd wouldn't
prefer a life of ease in my court, she smiled,
curtsied her gratitude for the honour
I'd bestowed upon her, but declared
herself content with her station in life.

Being a gentleman, I had to respect
her wish, but couldn't understand
why she'd prefer a traveler's lot
to the lolling one I offered.

When I asked the leader of the troupe
if she might be persuaded to spend
a night in my tent, he stammered
like an axe striking unyielding heart wood,
that the lady was spoken for,
besotted by the band's clown and lutenist.

I contemplated having the jongleur
removed, one way or another,
but decided against it, though a pity,
what a night she would've enjoyed.

Ophelia, as Cunegunde, Thinks of Fortinbras

Midway between boy and man,
he once stuttered admiration for me,
visiting Elsinore with his father,
the King of Norway, before war
clashed like two rearing chargers,
between our kingdoms.

So I feared he'd now call me,
"Lady Ophelia," and give away
the secret I'd kept from the others.

But he only bowed, kissed my hand
and kept holding it,
as if it contained some magical charm,
perhaps suspecting I wasn't
saucy Cunegunde,
or maybe still tongue-tied
at what his child's eyes
had perceived as a shining beauty,
though I never saw myself
as one to make men sigh
out their love or arouse in them
ungovernable passion.

When he regained his senses,
he asked if I'd not prefer court ease
to the toil of a strolling player.
The implication? As his mistress.

"I'm content here, My Lord,
but thank you for giving me
the great honour of asking,"
and curtsied as prettily
as my serving maids
when I granted their requests
for an evening alone,
to entertain their chosen swain
of the hour, in a dark corner
of the court's gardens.

But I had all I needed
and wanted in our troupe,
except the fear I'd be found out
as Ophelia, not the Cunegunde
they've all, save Feste, believe me to be.

I begin to wonder why I should keep
my identity hidden: all who could have
dragged me back to Elsinore are dead:
my poor father and brother among them,
as is dread Hamlet and that usurping
murderer, Claudius.

Still, always best to be careful,
no telling who might accuse me of what,
were I to reveal my true identity.

Isaak, Another Member of the Troupe of Traveling Players

Ever since we left Elsinore
Cunegunde's changed:
where once if she'd see me
carrying logs for our fires,
she'd trip me and laugh,

"Clumsy Jew!" Now, she helps.

And when she'd stumble
over her lines,
as if on slippery river rocks,
she'd bare her bosoms,
or if more desperate
to have forgotten a line
or to gain a cheap laugh,
she'd lift her kirtle's hems
for just an instant,
revealing her dark forest—
to lusty hoots of joy
and flung kronor.

Now, she has no patience
to play the slut with our audiences,
nor with our leader, Gunnar,
who wears a face of rancid milk.
Instead, she'll sit with Feste,
and if she thinks no one's watching,
will kiss him.

And when she once recently
came upon me in a glade,
saw me binding the prayer boxes
to my left arm and forehead,
she didn't sneer, but asked,
polite as a schoolgirl, why.

I explained Jews are required
to wear them while reciting
the articles of our faith:
that the Lord is our God,
the Lord is One.

Others of our troupe claim
she's Lady Ophelia of Elsinore,
not Cunegunde at all,
and suspect she did away
with the bawd, and though
there is a resemblance,
my old eyes and heart want
to believe she's Cunegunde,
magically transformed
into a true Woman of Valor,

but in my soul, I know the truth.

Samson, the Traveling Acting Troupe's Strongman

Cunegunde? Dull as an ox
that I am, I can tell
she's some other beauty.
Folk don't change from
cruel to kind for no reason.

When we performed in Elsinore,
I caught a glimpse brief
as a panicked hare,
of Ophelia, a court lady,
before she retired
to her chamber.

God's Blood, she bore
our little whore and minx
such a resemblance
as stopped my breath.

The two must've traded places,
and Cunegunde, not Ophelia,
who drowned: Cunegunde,
who could think of no greater fun
than taunting me with a show
of her golden titties.

Still, I'll mourn the vixen;
when Gunnar was away arranging
our performance in Elsinore,
she granted me entry past the gates
of her moist heaven: Gunnar,
she complained, never
tupping her to her satisfaction.

"Don't be too gentle," she purred,
her legs gripping me like ivy
on a castle wall,
until she shrieked her finish.

But as she was rearranging
her kirtle, her voice went cold
and hard as the ice of Ultima Thule,
not to expect that gift ever again.

"I won't jeopardize
my place with Gunnar,
for the likes of you,"
she sneered, and me still
basking in that paradise
I'd been lent, then seen
snatched away.

I'd wager she'd have changed
her tune had she lived,
though more likely
I'd be expelled from our troupe,
and she'd be left untouched,
for fear of ruining her value
with the men in the audience,
if I were to let it drop to Gunnar
how frisky she was with not just me,
but all the men in our company.

Not worth the wager
of tattling on her,
and also, no one deserves
the end she suffered.

Isaak Remembers What Drew Him to the Actor's Life

A troupe visited our *shtetl*
when I was ten, and though Papa
forbade me to watch "That *trayf*"
of doors slamming,
cuckolded husbands shouting,
rogues paddling those buffoons'
buttocks, I roared.

From that afternoon,
Papa's carpentry shop
was the Babylonian Captivity,
no longer a cedar-fragrant Garden.

So one night, after Papa slapped me
for being a lazy dreamer, I was off.
When I caught up with the troupe,
apparent, even, alas, to me,
I was hopeless as a stroller,
worse as a jongleur.

I could, however, fix anything:
something I'd learned from Papa,
helping him build chairs,
tables, cabinets, and coffins.

So I repair sets and wagon wheels,
get paid to watch the plays for free!
And who's as handy as me?
Gunnar? He couldn't hammer
his thumb, let alone a nail.

When *I daven,* he shrugs,
"Who's to say which god is right?"
I repay him by listening
and tsking sympathy when he laments
Cunegunde no longer rolls
naked in his featherbed.

"Women," I shrug,
"I can't understand them,
except for my mother.
All she wanted
was her little darling boy
tied to her apron strings,
and rubbing her sore feet
of an evening, forever."

Of course, I wouldn't dream
of telling him or anyone else
in our troupe, that Cunegunde
is really Lady Ophelia.

Let them figure it out
for themselves, and besides
a lady without secrets
is a very dull lady indeed.

Ophelia, as Cunegunde, Considers Isaak

Though Isaak has said nothing
about how Cunegunde and I
looked like twins—she as wild
to play the great Court lady
as I to escape Hamlet's scorpion
tongue—he's pierced my secret.

"Don't worry," he assured me
and held my soft hand as tenderly
as a man who's worked with hammer
and nails all his life, can,
"I'll tell no one."

How I want to believe that he won't
demand kronor not to return me
to Elsinore for a reward: his people
notorious for greed, or so I've heard.

If Feste and now Isaak have pierced
my secret, the others won't be far behind.
I'm not sure I can trust any of them,
especially Griselda, who shoots me looks
of such hate, a wonder they don't knock
me over with their bear-ferocity.

What I've done to earn her rage,
I've no idea, though I'll wager
Cunegunde was none too gentle
with her, and besides, Griselda
was probably jealous of the place
the bawdy wench had in Gunnar's heart,
or more to the point, his loins.

I recall how Cunegunde
had to be all but restrained,
like a fiery, runaway blooded mare,
from leaping on Hamlet:
not just for his being a prince,
but I'll give him this: a fine
looking man, when he wasn't
sneering or sulking, or trembling
with doubt over what to do
about King Claudius.

Now, Isaak smiles at me,
warm as a day in high summer,
calls me, "Bubbaleh," obviously
a term of affection among his tribe,
his hard hands soft as meadow flowers
dancing in a bathing breeze,
then quickly withdrawn

Yes, I can trust him.

Griselda Plots the Downfall of Ophelia

My face pasty-plain as dough,
my titties tiny as peach pits,
Gunnar paid me less attention
than he would a sliver
of smashed crockery:
too busy playing
the randy bull
with Cunegunde's
swaying hipped heifer.

I hate her for her soft curves,
her lush-as-satin lips,
her easy way with Gunnar,
in whose bed I'd gladly
have died, but the one time
he turned to me as if to
a desperate port in the storm
of lust that engulfs him,
he failed to raise his lateen
and blamed me
for not inspiring him enough.

Besides, he was besotted
with the slut, who made me
hop to her every whim,
until the troupe performed
the play that revealed
King Claudius' guilt.

After we left Elsinore,
she smiled at everyone,
did more than her share
of fetching, gathering wood,
cooking at our outdoor fires,
and never once lay in Gunnar's bed.

But she can't fool me,
she's biding her time
before letting Gunnar
have her again, false resistance
sweetening her honey pot,

while I gave him every sign
I was eager as a fawning hound,
at the chores a strolling troupe
has to carry out,
and in the minor roles
he deigned to let me take
and never gave me credit
for playing true to life.

When he did invite me
into his wagon to please him,
he slapped me for failing
to make his mast stand ready,
told me to leave and never return.

"Fetching and gathering
are your lot, my girl,"
he sneered, as I ran, sobbing,
back to my wind-ripped tent,
and have got hold of a potion
that'll make him choke and die.

I'll plant the empty vial
on Cunegunde's person
and watch her hang:
the troupe mine, to order about
and take the juiciest roles,
while she'll be tossed
into unhallowed,
crossroads ground,
for good Christians
to tread on and crush
her sinful bones.

Griselda and the Vial of Poison

This vial of vengeance
should be for Gunnar,
but I can't bring myself
to slip its frothing liquid
into his flagon,
even though he orders me
about like a serf,
me who worshipped him
as a nun loves Our Lord.

They say hell hath no fury
like a woman scorned,
even worse, one ignored:
my un-met passion
boiling into hate.
Still, I can't kill him
and blame Cunegunde.

So what's left for me?
Home? Endless toil,
beatings, Father sneering,
"No man will take you
with your toad's face!"
Mother? She pinched me,
mocked me for a jenny mule,
good only for hauling.

Or continue here, the dogs-body
of all, when I burn to perform.
At least Cunegunde now willingly
shares my chores, until, that is,
she'll return to her bitch-
princess ways.

But now, to my shock,
she bids me sit with her.

"You can play," she begins,
"every part as if born to each.
Fancy performing tonight?"

"Why?" my suspicions fly
like volleys of siege-arrows.
She glances at the swelling
beneath her kirtle, smiles,
shrugs, and sighs,

"The blessed child of Feste,
not, thank Our Kind Lady,
Hamlet's cursed issue,"
and takes my hand.

"You do know
I'm not Cunegunde.
We traded places in Elsinore.
I was once Hamlet's love,
then his whipped jenny.
Call me Ophelia."

"You fooled me," I laugh,
"and should've known
people don't change,
only become more themselves.
But what of my face?" I wail.

"That won't matter
after five well-spoken lines."

And suddenly, I'm sobbing gratitude,
that someone finally sees me.

Griselda Returns the Vial of Poison to the Crone

Not Cunegunde,
but rather, Lady Ophelia.
I cried gratitude when she assured me
how well I'd play her part.
But now I must dispose of
this vicious little phial,
its green liquid oozing death.

"I knew you'd be back,"
the crone cackles.
"My one surprise: you didn't
ask for a love potion—
though they seldom work.
Still, love-sick fools persist,"
she chortled.

"Poison's surer," I shrugged,
she nodded toothless agreement,
as if to invite me into her business.

But no, I was glad that venom
was out of my sweating hands.

III—Such Strength of Love

Gunnar Learns the Truth About the Woman He Thought Was Cunegunde

Her coldness finally clear:
not my bawdy Cunegunde,
murdered by mad Hamlet.
Were he still alive I'd kill
the royal wretch.

She's weepy Ophelia,
who'd traded places
with my beloved slut:
alike as twin lambs,
though Cunegunde
was a wolf of sacred lust.

When I told Isaak,
our carpenter, I'd barter
Ophelia to King Fortinbras
for a reward, the Jew roared
like his Old Book prophets,

"She came to us a suppliant!
Have you not heard of Ruth?
Nor read your own Book?
Besides, audiences reward
her excellence upon the boards
with showers of kronor!"

"Think," I argued,
"how much she'd fetch.
And now, with a child
by Feste on its way,
she'll be useless for weeks,
perhaps months.

"Besides, Cunegunde,
my poor dead darling,
couldn't deliver a two-word aside,
without getting three words wrong,
but she bewitched the punters
to empty their purses,
when she flaunted
her fuck-lovely breasts!"

"May *Hashem* strike you down
for this sin of greed!"
Isaak's curse a thunderclap
of freezing rain slashing down
on a moor-lost wretch.

Still, without telling the Jew,
I'll trade her to Fortinbras,
who clearly was smitten,
easy to find a new wanton
to stumble over her lines,
and bare her opulent breasts
and grant my shafted orisons
on my feather bed.

"Boy," I summon an apprentice,
"take this sealed missive
to King Fortinbras.
Await his answer and return."

Fortinbras Confronts Ophelia

What a cunning vixen you are!
To have me believe
you were Cunegunde,
when our paths crossed
after you'd escaped Elsinore's
blood-polluted kingdom,
now my duchy.

A shame, madman-Hamlet
slew your delectable double:
what a loss of a true devotee
to the goddess of lust
was her passing.
A shame, too, you refused
my offer: a life of leisurely
dalliance in my court.

But now that I see you
in your true aspect, I'm agape
not just at your beauty,
but at your cleverness;
not many can best me
with ploys and wiles.

When we met as children,
I thought you beautiful,
though too much
like stained glass
shattering in a storm.

You're slyer now,
a minx to reckon with,
so while your Gunnar
offers to sell you to me,
I'd never force you.

But I will ask again:
be my concubine;
we'll please each other
until I find a suitably royal wife,
and perhaps even after
I take my lawful queen.

You'll advise me
on how to speak to
and handle my subjects,
courtiers, allies, and foes.

Or, if you're still bent
on living wild and free,
what other gift
can I present to you?

Ophelia Rejects the Offer of King Fortinbras

My Lord, you do me
too great an honour.
Were I not tainted
by the curse of Elsinore,
I'd gladly accept
your condescending
to make me your bedmate
and councilor.

But Denmark was so corrupt
it cursed me as well:
between Claudius's murder
of the old king and young Hamlet's
madness that unleashed chaos
and more murders
of so many notables
that I can't count them all,
though I particularly mourn
my dear brother, Laertes,
and my darling Papa, Polonius,
killed by the Demon Prince
as a sort of vicious whim.

Even more, your subjects
and clerics would reject me,
for being the illicit consort
to Hamlet the Mad,
who cursed all he touched.
Your courtiers and advisers
would howl outrage
should you bring me in tow,
heavy with Hamlet's child.
You'd face open rebellion.

Your gift to me?
Allow me my self-exile
among these harmless players,
to make something useful of my life,
not an idle creature of the Court.
Find a more deserving consort,
someone not polluted
by Hamlet's poisoned seed.

So I fear, my dear Liege,
we must set aside
our mutual desires,
so that you might continue
to thrive as monarch of Norway
and now of Denmark.
But know you'll always
warmly reside in my heart
and that I will follow
your ever-more brilliant reign
with assiduous interest,
rejoicing in your victories.

May they be many and great!

But if I may beg one more boon,
I should like to see the back
of Gunnar and his cunning.
Time for him to leave our troupe
in more honest hands,
like myself and the jongleur Feste.

We have been watching
as Gunnar has run our band
into the ground;
time for new hands and ideas
to take over our troupe.

Ophelia, After Rejecting the Suit of King Fortinbras

It took all my acting skill
to make Fortinbras believe
this child I carry is Hamlet's,
though I'd expelled that creature
before I set off to be a strolling player.

It's darling Feste's issue inside me,
kicking lustily as a minstrel trilling
his first melodies to the grateful world.

Luckily, Fortinbras believed me,
and accepted my false regrets.
Why would I exchange my strolling-
player's life—with its tossed coins
and applause wild as storm-
dancing birches, in every town—
to endure the yawning boredom
of Fortinbras, a ninny with as much wit
as a butcher's stall, but like all kings
imagining he's the fount of all things clever?

I've had my fill of scorpion-court
intrigues, of stale ripostes
to win the King's amused pat
on the head, as if for a cur
performing tricks
a wolf would never stoop to.

Townsfolk we play for ask,
horrified, yet fascinated,
how we can live in the open,
slapped by rain, sleet, and snow,
when they're prisoners
under their thatch, their tiny
windows smudged blind,
from their smoky peat fires,
when nothing's so grand
as viewing the great wheel
of the stars and the moon's
silver glow, more entertaining
than even our best performances.

One winter midnight,
Feste and I gaped and gasped
at the Lights weaving tapestries
in snake-sinuous greens and crimsons,
while he spun tales of true lovers
and of the child who will bless our union.

Why would I give up the balm
of breathing God's good air
for a palace fetid with stenches rising
from the Garterobe and the jakes:
the shit of royal and commoner
stinking the same?

Besides, Fortinbras is such
a swaggering ass: he stumbled
into Elsinore when no one
was manning its ramparts,
and boasted he'd won a victory
surpassing Caesar's against
the battle-fierce Gauls.

Ophelia Counsels Griselda, After the Latter's First Performance in the Strolling Troupe

You've the stroller's art
your diction clear,
your comic timing perfection,
your soliloquy had me in tears,
your entrances and exits
exact as the thrusts
of a stage swordsman,
you hit your cues and marks
as true as Master Brahe's
astronomical measurements.

But can I advise you
on a different matter?
Forgive my candor and meddling,
but I see how you've switched
your longing from Gunnar
onto our strongman, Samson,
who hardly notices you at all.

All your life, you've been told
you're no beauty, so you believe
that canard. The truth?
With a little care for your attire,
the substitution of a smile
for your scowl of dashed hopes
bitter as a dose of wolfbane,

with a necklace to accentuate
your lovely throat,
you'll have Samson groveling,
spouting eloquent oratories
of his love, to earn him the prize
you've sought, and him none the wiser.

King Fortinbras to Gunnar

It seems, sirrah,
both you and I were denied
Ophelia's secret garden—
the lady's petals
wrapped 'round Feste,
your troupe's clown
and lutenist: the luckiest
fool in Our kingdom.

If We were a worm-mealy
monarch, We'd order
his head removed, but kings,
as well as commoners,
must be gracious losers
in the carnal game.

Should We hear
you've tried to have her,
by bribe or blackmail—
for her heart is decided—
there's no place
in Our Great Kingdom
you can escape to.

She has suffered too much
from a prince's viper tongue,
having to sham her drowning
and take up with you
and your players,
to escape his verbal venom

We regard the lady
too highly as a paragon
to allow your lecheries,
though We knew her apologies
in denying Our offer
of concubinage—
for marriage is impossible
with one not of the royal line—
were meant to assuage
my regal self-regard.

As for selling her to me,
I will not sanction
your role as Panderus.
It's time you tried
some other line of work,
and leave the lady
and her true paramour
to lead the acting troupe
your chicaneries were ruining.

Now, find a suitable wench
of your own station,
to pour your heart
and seed into.

Gunnar, After Being Confronted by King Fortinbras

The King needn't have glared
and threatened to remove my head,
for me to forsake Ophelia,
who duped me by passing for
Cunegunde, the two as alike
in face and form as fern fronds.

But after we were waylaid
a second time by Fortinbras
and his courtiers, and after
his closeted talk with Ophelia,
and after she revealed herself
to the troupe, like the heroine
of a stage comedy, and after the King
warned me off her, for the love
he bore her as children,

I decided the stroller's life
was not such a paragon after all.
Indeed, I've found a wealthy
tavern owner-widow: Merry Portia
eager for my maypole.

Now, no haggling over wages
with players who believe
our troupe would collapse
without their fret and strut,
no more wagon wheels snapping
and needing to be repaired
before we can continue
to our next engagement,
no players snarling, for receiving
fewer lines than some others.

Let the troupe's new leaders—
Ophelia and her lutenist-love,
Feste—worry about such fripperies;
it's time for me to rest and enjoy
the fruits of a well-earned marriage.

Samson Thinks of Griselda

Once upon a very bad time,
she was a sharp-toothed shrew,
for not being allowed on stage
by Gunnar, who sneered
her face was hard as a knothole,
her figure a splintery slat of wood,

thus unfit to strut the boards,
while his favorite, Cunegunde,
who couldn't recite three words in a row,
flaunted her perfect titties on stage
whenever she flubbed her lines,
and so was touted by Gunnar
as our greatest acting asset.

But now that Gunnar's left us
for a rich tavern widow's
pillow breasts and bags of kronor,
and Ophelia and Feste lead
our troupe, and our greedy
Cunegunde is dead, Griselda glows
like rush candles lighting up the roles

Ophelia pens for her, and smiles wide
as a palace ballroom, her life no longer
a misery of hauling, cooking, and serving
the rest of our troupe, before she's allowed
to gnaw like a stray, on gristle and bones.

At our noon meal today, her fingers
laced into mine, and such a smile
she graced me with, to outshine
our glorious, northern midsummer sun.

Griselda Thinks of Samson

I wasted years adoring Gunnar,
who wanted me only when the woman
he thought Cunegunde could no longer
abide his bed or his mast, which failed
to hold steady and strong that one time.
But when at last, I knew all he really wanted
was Cunegunde's ripe figure under him,
not caring she dropped her lines
like a kitchen maid spilling ale flagons,
my love turned to wintry hate.

I thank Our Lady of Forgiveness
I didn't poison him and try to blame
Ophelia, whom I took for Cunegunde:
the one desperate to escape Elsinore's rot
and stink, the other dying—alas all too true—
to play the great court lady, the two
as alike in countenance as pine combs,

except where Cunegunde was haughty
as a queen, Ophelia wanted only to be useful
and liked by everyone, I alone thinking
she had to be a hypocrite. But once
she and Feste took over our troupe,
she was kind to me, for no reason,
except her good nature: letting me perform
in her place, even penning new roles for me,
knowing I'd been thwarted by Gunnar;
his one test for a female stroller:
brazening ripe bosoms for tossed-on-stage kronor.

All the time I'd puppy-dogged after him,
I sneered at our strongman, Samson,
thought his only skills, to lift heavy objects
and slam down the arms of other men
in arm wrestling competitions.

But after Gunnar left for his rich tavern widow,
I heard Samson singing while he sewed a patch
on a jerkin, his voice sweet as a wren's,
his fingers deft as a swallow weaving the sky.

And when he looked up at me, his wasn't
the face of a brute, but of a man in love.

Ophelia Considers Her New Life

Strange, the turns a life can take:
I've gone from Hamlet's fawn-frail prey;
to trading places with Cunegunde
and performing for audiences;
and now, to leading our troupe with Feste,
when Gunnar decamped
for a tavern-widow's feather-soft breasts
and all the ale he could swill,
our band the better for Sir Bombast
taking his swaggering leave,
more a well-oiled wagon hub now:

My love, Feste—our clown,
lutenist, and now dramatic lead—
troubadours our arrivals,
to lift lives drab as the mud
most of our audience mucks
into sparse crops,
so we'll often perform
for meals and a hayloft.
No softer bed for Feste and me
and the child that will soon
be our bright-eyed blessing,
to find Heaven in, a little ways
above the dirt of this earth.

Our strongman Samson bargains
for provisions, few eager to face
his grim silence and bear-trap fists,
should they refuse his cheapening,
or try to gouge him like an awl
punching holes in leather.
Also, he shows a surprising skill
at playing against type in comedies.

And Griselda, who once Gunnar scoffed at
for a donkey-face, is a miracle:
her lines spoken so true to life,
her visage so saint-comely when she acts,
I scribble new roles for her.
Last but far from least, Isaak,
our Hebrew carpenter: nothing
he can't mend or build;
but laughing, the first to admit
a wall would be a more supple actor.

At dawn and dusk he prays to his *Hashem*.
May his God watch over us all. Amen.

About the Author

Robert Cooperman confesses that *Macbeth,* not *Hamlet,* is his favorite play by Shakespeare. In fact, *The Death and Rebirth of Ophelia* is his revenge on the play for having been forced to read it on all-too numerous occasions in high school, college, and graduate school, and has come to thoroughly detest the title character. So, one fine day the thought hit him over the head: What if Ophelia traded places with a woman who bore her an uncanny resemblance in the visiting acting troupe and left Elsinore with that troupe, to become a strolling player? Such is the premise of Cooperman's latest poetry collection.

In the past, he's written about the Trojan War and its aftermath—*The Ghosts and Bones of Troy* (Kelsay Books, 2020), *Lost on the Blood Dark Sea* (FutureCycle Press, 2020), and *Troy* (March Street Press, 2011)—especially from the point of view of his first literary hero, Odysseus.

Other collections have followed Cooperman's hyper-violent Old West alter ego, John Sprockett, "that saint of sacred mayhem," who will never allow a lady to be scorned or anyone to stare rudely at his ruined face, as in *In the Colorado Gold Fever Mountains* (Western Reflections Pub Co., 1999), *The Widow's Burden* (Western Reflections Pub Co., 2001), and *A Nightmare on Horseback* (Kelsay Books, 2022).

Most recently, in *Steerage* (Kelsay Books, 2024), he created a highly fictionalized account of his maternal grandfather's youthful travails on the Lower East Side of Manhattan in the early 20th century. *Draft Board Blues* (FutureCycle Press, 2017), another recent collection, narrated Cooperman's battle to keep from being killed in Vietnam. *Their Wars* (Kelsay Books, 2018) tells of his parents' experiences at then Fort Bragg during the last days of World War II.

Cooperman grew up in Brooklyn, New York, and completed a PhD in Creative Writing and 19th-century British Literature at the University of Denver. He has taught at the University of Georgia, Bowling Green State University, and the University of Baltimore.

He lives in Denver with his wife Beth.

www.ingramcontent.com/pod-product-compliance
Lightning Source LLC
Chambersburg PA
CBHW030052170426
43197CB00010B/1488